KIDS UNPLUGGED

OCEAN QUEST

ACTIVITY BOOK

WRITTEN AND ILLUSTRATED BY

FELICITY FRENCH

PETER PAUPER PRESS, INC.
WHITE PLAINS, NEW YORK

PETER PAUPER PRESS
Fine Books and Gifts Since 1928

In 1928, at the age of twenty-two, Peter Beilenson began printing books on a small press in the basement of his parents' home in Larchmont, New York. Peter—and later, his wife, Edna—sought to create fine books that sold at "prices even a pauper could afford."

Today, still family owned and operated, Peter Pauper Press continues to honor our founders' legacy of quality, value, and fun for big kids and small kids alike.

Illustrations © Felicity French

Copyright © 2016 Peter Pauper Press, Inc.
Manufactured for Peter Pauper Press, Inc.
202 Mamaroneck Avenue,
White Plains, NY, USA 10601

ISBN 978-1-4413-1997-5

Printed in China

Published in the United Kingdom and Europe by
Peter Pauper Press, Inc. c/o White Pebble International
Unit 2, Plot 11 Terminus Road
Chichester, West Sussex PO19 8TX, UK

7 6 5 4 3 2

Visit us at www.peterpauper.com

Ahoy!

Did you know that oceans cover more than 70 percent of our planet? It's true! The five oceans are vast and full of exciting mysteries we have yet to explore. And in the parts we have explored, amazing forms of sealife have thrived for over a hundred million years. For example, have you ever heard of the anglerfish, a deep-sea creature that uses a light dangling from its head to lure prey right into its toothy jaws? And then there's the blue whale, the largest animal known to have ever existed, which has a tongue as heavy as an elephant!

In these pages, you'll find plenty of fintastic facts like these along with brain-teasing games, cool coloring pages and crafts, and immense underwater worlds waiting to be filled with ocean critters. So test your brain power and imagination as you ride the waves to fun times.

LET YOUR CREATIVITY FLOW AND SET SAIL FOR AN UNDERWATER ADVENTURE! NO WIRES REQUIRED!

ANSWERS ARE IN THE BACK OF THE BOOK.

oceans of the world

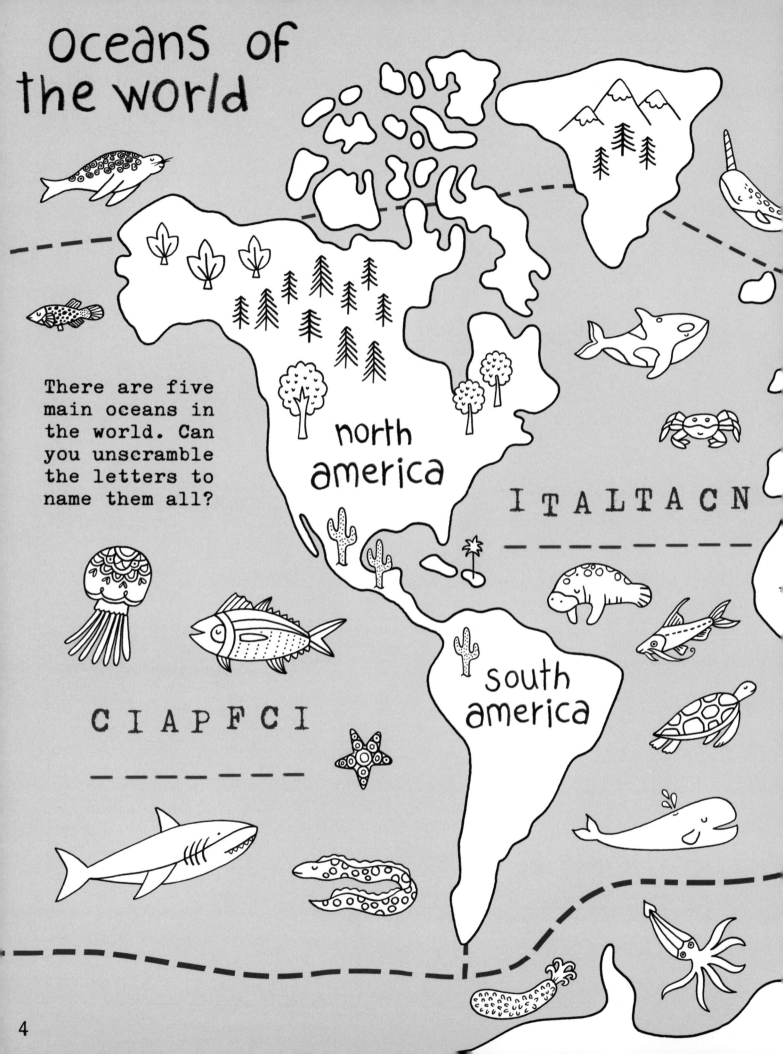

There are five main oceans in the world. Can you unscramble the letters to name them all?

north america

south america

ITALTACN
- - - - - - -

CIAPFCI
- - - - - -

C A R I T C

_ _ _ _ _ _

Can you find all of these ocean dwellers on the map?

asia

blackfish	orca	
blue whale	penguin	
catfish	polar bear	squid
clownfish	ringed seal	starfish
crab	sea anemone	tuna
dolphin	sea cucumber	turtle
eel	sea otter	walrus
harp seal	sea urchin	
jellyfish	seahorse	
krill	shark	
manatee	sperm whale	
narwhal		

europe

africa

I D N N I A

_ _ _ _ _

australia

H S O E U T R N

_ _ _ _ _

antarctica

5

Fill the sea with boats and leaping dolphins, and decorate the lighthouse with different patterns. Then color it all in!

DESIGN YOUR OWN
TREASURE MAP

Fill your map
with islands, trees,
mountains, volcanoes,
beaches, ships,
and sea creatures.

Remember, X marks
the spot!

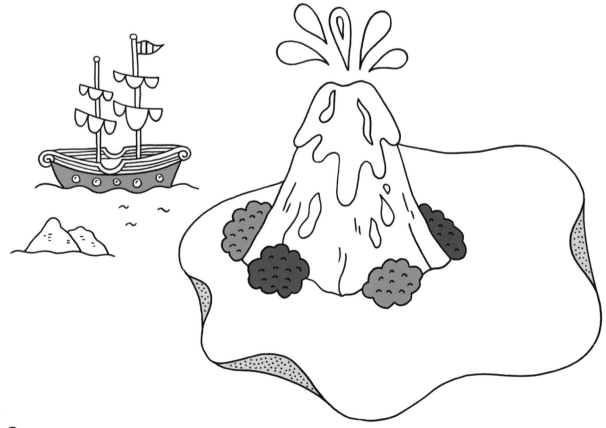

Making Waves

Fill the scene with swirling blue waves and beautiful boats, then color them in.

Fill the turtle shells with lots of patterns, and draw wavy blue lines for the sea.

DID YOU KNOW?
Turtles have existed for at least 220 million years. They were around when dinosaurs roamed the Earth!

13

COLORFUL CRABS

Color this patterned crab in shades of red and orange. On the next page, use the body as a starting point to draw your own crab!

Draw dots with a marker to fill the beach with sand.

Make your own
SAND ORNAMENTS

YOU WILL NEED:
Wax paper, pencil, craft glue, sand, string, template or cookie cutter

1. Draw your shape onto wax paper with a pencil. You can draw around a cookie cutter or use one of the templates on the opposite page.

2. Go around the outline of your shape with craft glue.

3. Now fill in the rest of your shape with glue.

4. Sprinkle sand all over your shape and then leave for 24-36 hours to dry.

String

5. When it is dry, it should peel easily off the wax paper. Ask an adult to make a hole in the top of your shape, then thread your string through and hang it up!

Lay wax paper on top and draw around these templates to make your sand ornaments.

17

Decorate and color these beautiful shells.

Color these starfish, then use the next page to create your own patterns.

DID YOU KNOW?

There are over 2,000 kinds of starfish (also known as sea stars), and they live in every ocean on Earth. Starfish come in many different colors and patterns, and most have spiky surfaces which help protect them from predators like fish, sea otters, and birds. The most well-known starfish have five arms, but some have many more. The sun star can have up to forty arms!

SEA URCHINS

Complete these sea urchins so they
are symmetrical, meaning both sides
look the same. Then color them in.

DID YOU KNOW?

There are around 1,000 species of sea urchin in the world. They live in every ocean on Earth and can be found on the seabed near coral reefs.

SUPER SEA SPONGES

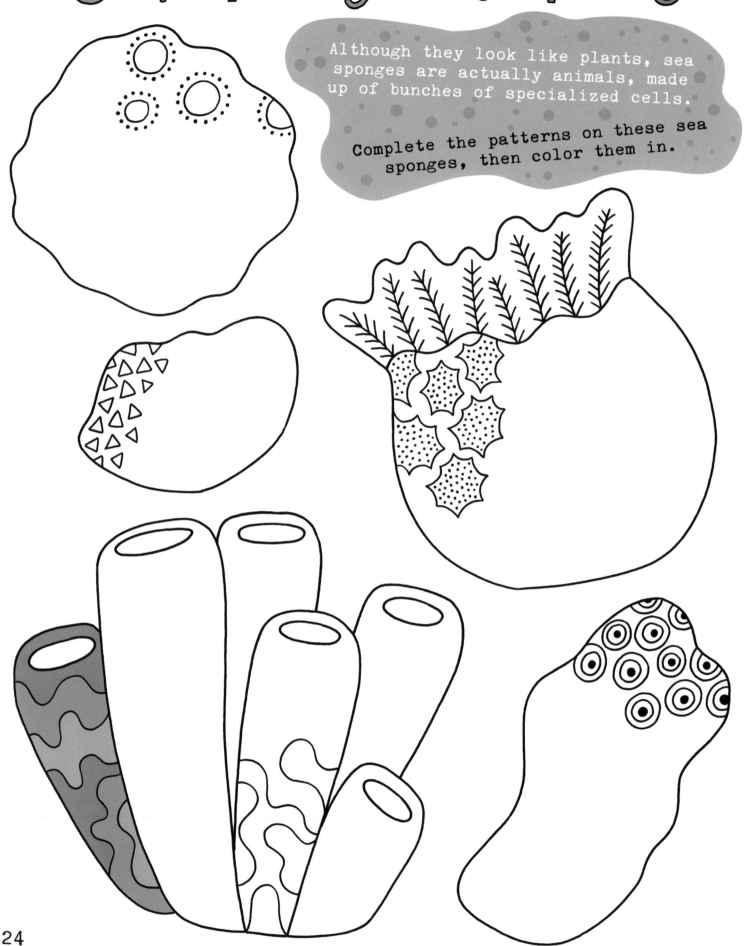

Although they look like plants, sea sponges are actually animals, made up of bunches of specialized cells.

Complete the patterns on these sea sponges, then color them in.

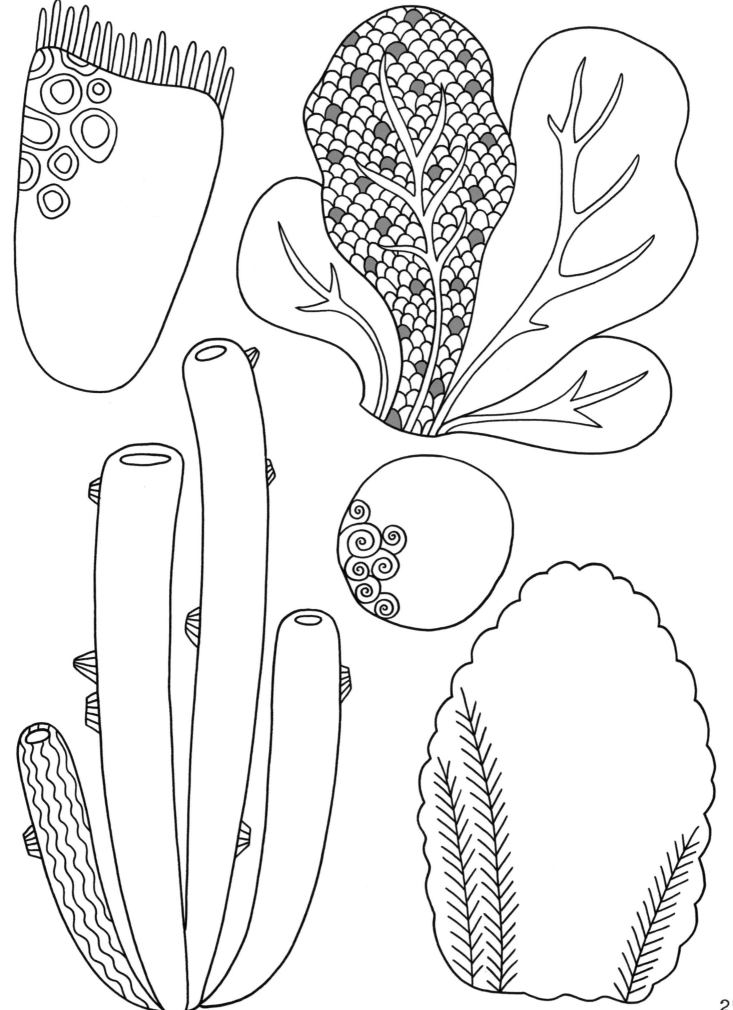

These
clownfish
are hiding
among the coral.
Use the key to
color them in!

PEARLS OF WISDOM

This oyster is hiding a rare natural gem. Follow the maze to find the precious pearl.

START

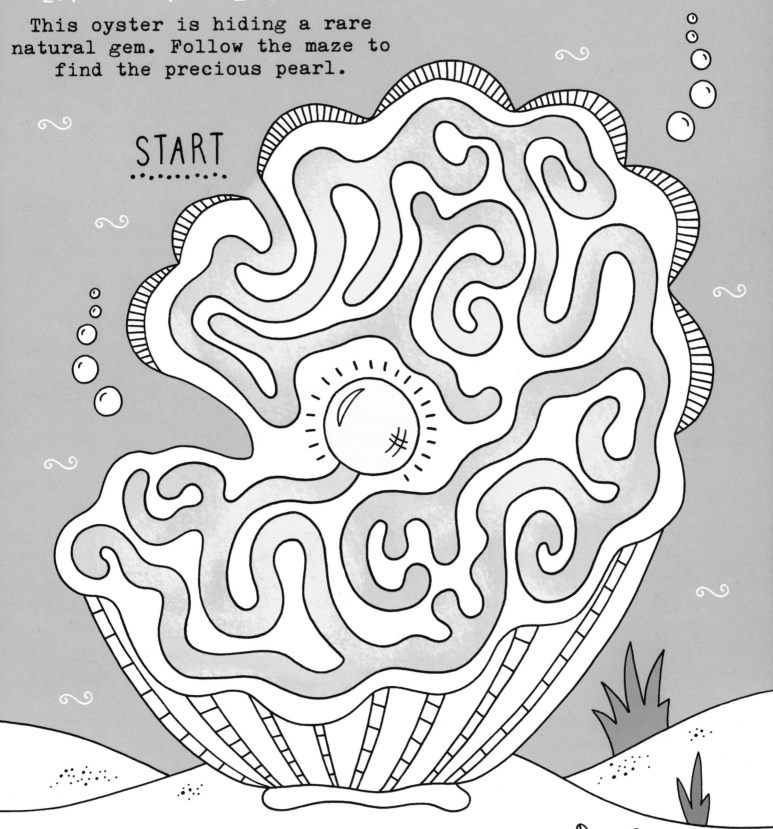

Pearls are formed when a foreign object, like a piece of sand or coral, makes its way inside the shell of an oyster. To protect itself, the oyster covers the object with a layer of a substance called nacre. Over time the layers of nacre build up to form a beautiful pearl.

WHALES OF THE WORLD

Whales don't breathe through their mouths. Instead they breathe through blowholes on the tops of their heads! As they surface, whales exhale explosively in a gush of misty air (called a blow), then breathe in before diving.

Draw blows coming from all of the whales' blowholes as they breathe out.

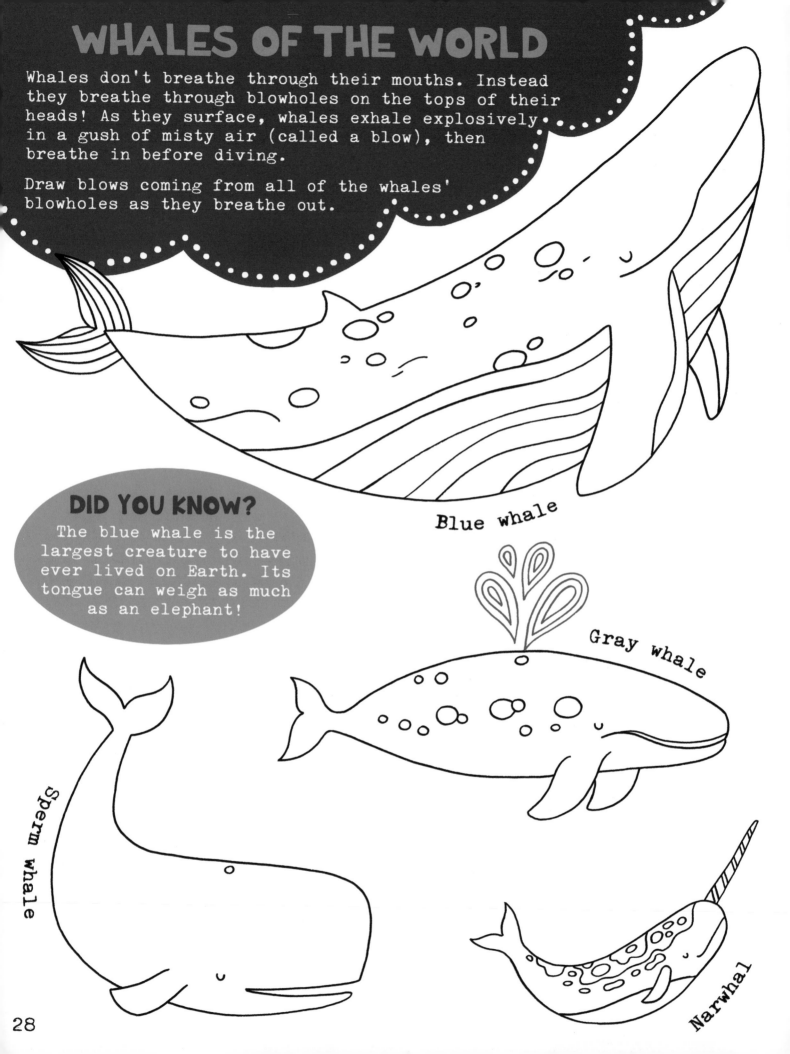

Blue whale

DID YOU KNOW?

The blue whale is the largest creature to have ever lived on Earth. Its tongue can weigh as much as an elephant!

Gray whale

Sperm whale

Narwhal

Decorate and color these
impressive sea creatures.

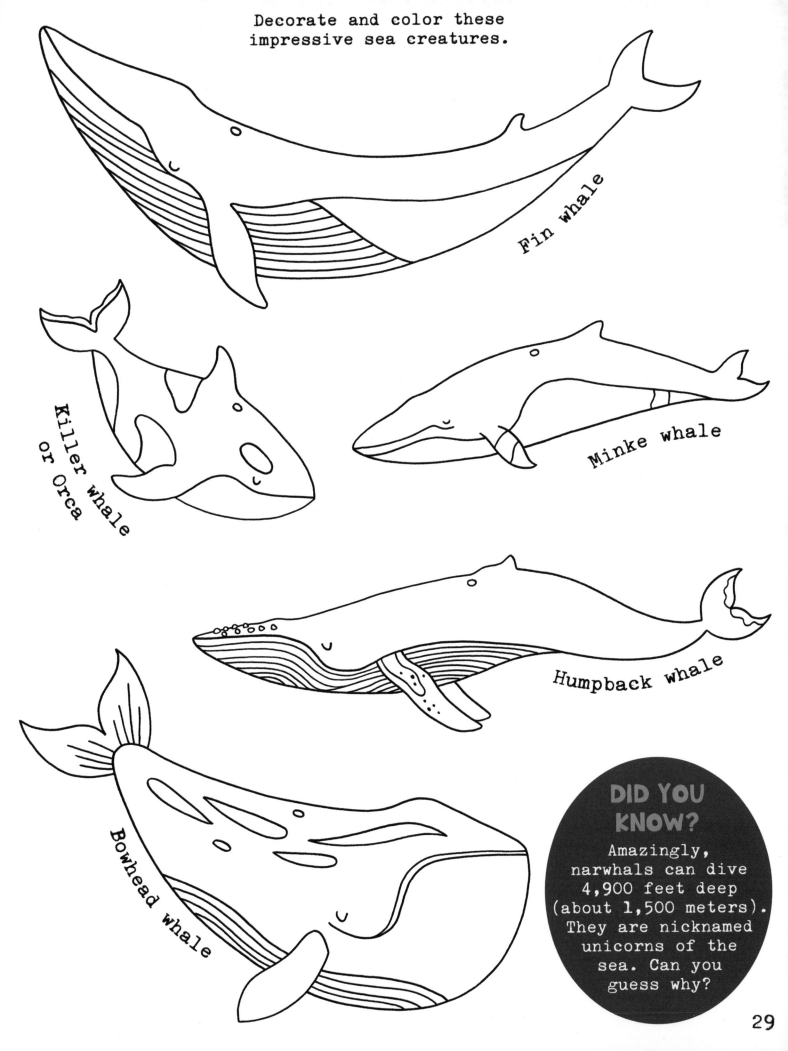

Fin whale

Killer whale
or Orca

Minke whale

Humpback whale

Bowhead whale

DID YOU KNOW?

Amazingly,
narwhals can dive
4,900 feet deep
(about 1,500 meters).
They are nicknamed
unicorns of the
sea. Can you
guess why?

WHALE WORD SEARCH

Can you find all of these whale-related words in the puzzle below? Look up, down, forward, backward, and diagonally!

baleen
beluga
blowhole
blubber
blue
bowhead
dolphin
endangered
fin
flipper
gray

humpback
killer
krill
mammal
marine
minke
narwhal
orca
pilot
plankton
porpoise

```
F X A R P T L Y G O P R N A R W H A L S
K H J E M Q Q T P M L E Y S O M P Z H T
I E P L L I X Z A A A P B N V O N A N M
N E E L A B N H A Z N P L Q I Q L J P M
X F M I Q E U K Q C K I U P G F R E T O
P F R K Y M C B E A T L E Q F C Z I V N
G Y U N P O L I L B O F V T Q R K A C T
H H U B H U N A Q O N E S I O P R O P H
J X A G W I T W M L W J I R C M Z G I I
S C V J H L B B J M V H C Y A A P A E I
K H K P L Q I I O J A A O S G R E G A B
R C L I C A N L Q W Z M D L G I P I E S
A O R P I L O T E R H Y V X E N Y L X P
D K W O N M L L J W E E M W Y E U U C B
F E N D A N G E R E D B A P H G C P E G
B H N I U N C D I K W Q B D A I W M D Z
T P T R L M P U J A E R D U U Y V R I A
P Q B K U B Y I S Y A R G O L R P P G E
S U J B T V W R T K M E K K X B W Q S D
B Y U H P M U O I X T H K Y E R U R S D
```

How many krill can you count on this page? ◯

PAIR THE PLANKTON

Each plankton has a match, except one! Can you match them all up and find the odd one out? Color them as you go until you have found all the matching pairs!

DID YOU KNOW?

Plankton are mostly microscopic organisms made up of tiny plants and animals. They drift along the ocean currents and are an important source of food for many animals, including the largest animal of all—the blue whale.

Match the Mackerel

Here is a shoal of fish, each one different from the next, except two! Can you find the two fish that look exactly alike?

Once you've spotted them, color them in with beautiful matching colors so they stand out! Then color the rest of the fish.

DID YOU KNOW?
A group of fish is called a shoal, but if they're moving together in the same direction, they become a school.

GLASS JAR AQUARIUM

YOU WILL NEED:
- One clean glass jar with screw-on lid
- Aquarium gravel or small rocks
- Plastic aquarium plants
- Small plastic fish or sea creatures
- Blue food coloring
- Water

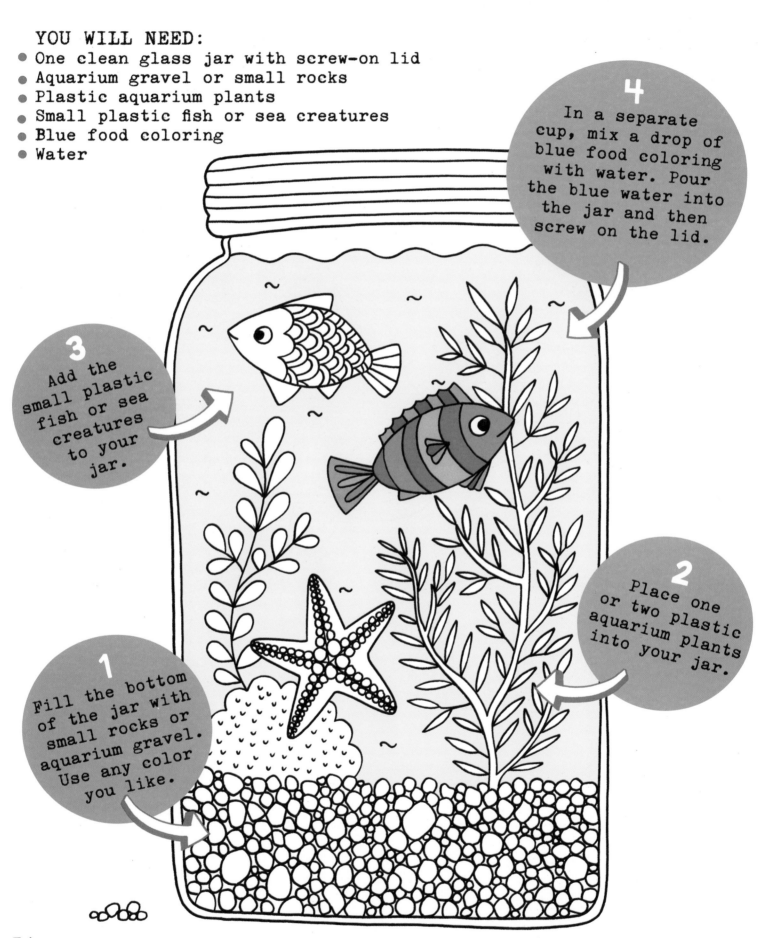

4 In a separate cup, mix a drop of blue food coloring with water. Pour the blue water into the jar and then screw on the lid.

3 Add the small plastic fish or sea creatures to your jar.

2 Place one or two plastic aquarium plants into your jar.

1 Fill the bottom of the jar with small rocks or aquarium gravel. Use any color you like.

Draw your finished aquarium here!

Draw your own school of fish.

GONE FISHING

Color this shark and fill the rest
of the sea with fish.

There's an animal hiding in the depths! Connect the dots to reveal the hidden creature!

Unscramble the letters to name this animal.

O E R E S
H A S S

_ _ _ _ _ _ _ _ _

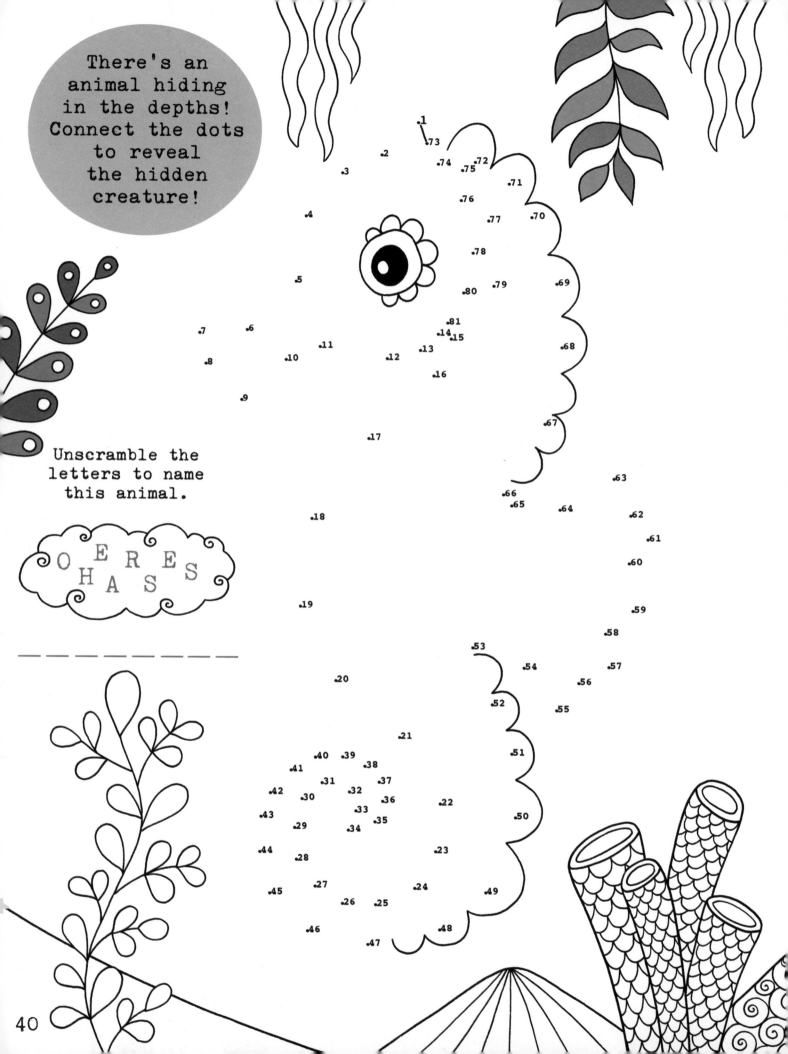

Fill the rest of the page with
these beautiful sea creatures,
then color it all in.

These animals have long, thin snouts which they use to get food out of tight places. They suck their food up like a vacuum cleaner!

Jazzy Jellies!

Color these pretty, patterned jellyfish in blues, purples, pinks, and greens.

DID YOU KNOW?

Some jellyfish are brightly colored, and some are nearly transparent, or see-through. This means some of them are nearly invisible to the human eye!

How many bubbles can you count on this page?

Jazz up these jellies by designing patterns on their bodies, adding tentacles, and coloring them in.

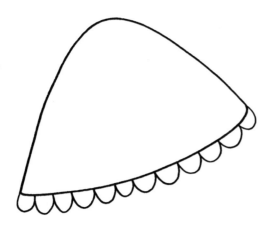

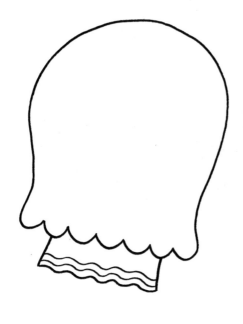

DEEP SEA DIVING

Draw yourself as a deep sea diver
surrounded by all of your favorite
ocean creatures. Then color it all in!

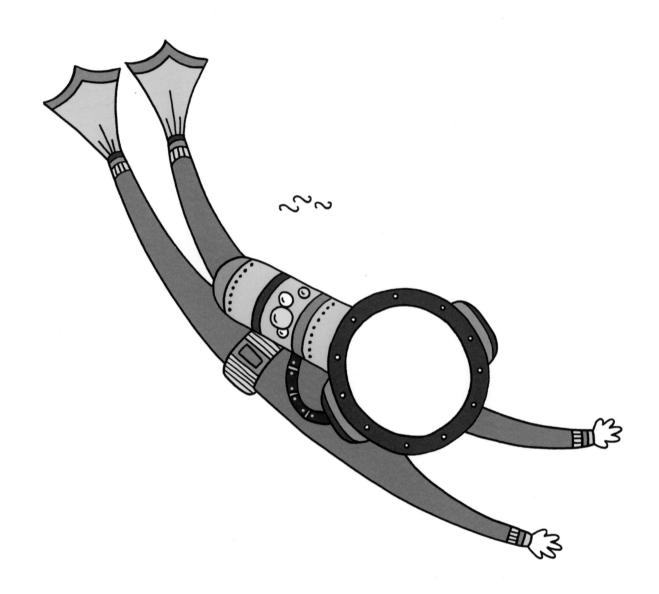

Fill this scene with plants, coral, shells,
and underwater volcanoes.

Find all these sea
creatures in the
treasure chest
on the next page.

angelfish
catfish
clownfish
cod
coral
crab
dolphin
eel
jellyfish
krill
lobster
mackerel

manatee
marlin
narwhal
octopus
parrotfish
penguin
plankton
red snapper
salmon
sardine
sea lion
sea otter
seahorse

seal
shark
shrimp
squid
starfish
stingray
swordfish
tuna
turtle
urchin
walrus
whale

TREASURE HUNT

Look forward, backward,
up, down, and diagonally.
When you're done, color
this fishy scene.

```
S L S I Y W L Q R L F B Y J E D P B H N
X E H H X T P Y E H S I F N W O L C S I
S O A J R E S P D C S L F E F O A T I H
E U C H N I E X S N Y I R V L U N U F P
E Y P G O A M S N G A S F P E H K N L L
X N U O Q R T P A E L R A D S K T A E O
L I I J T I S I P J L L W I R C O D G D
N F Q D N C V E P O L A F H I O N D N Q
C T Z G R F O H E I M T H P A Q W Q A S
P K R T F A S Y R J A I T W E L Q S E L
Y A A C O I S K E C B L E R E K C A M O
Y I R U F C U L M A N A T E E D L N A B
W A L R U S L J K C S C O R A L U I R S
X U A J O Y F S E A O T T E R E K H L T
F T O S F T E K L T P Y X X P X C C I E
S N B I L L F M T C Z D K R A H S R N R
V C S R T Z O I C N O I L A E S X U A P
E H U R J N C H S U K U X L W U F J Y B
L X U R D V Z P T H X Q J Y P Z R B Q Z
M T I B Z U W J I C F S Z X M Y E I K A
```

49

UNDERWATER ATLANTIS

Add extra sea creatures to this mysterious lost city. Then color it in!

50

DID YOU KNOW?

Atlantis was a legendary island, written about by the Greek thinker Plato hundreds of years ago. It was said to have sunk beneath the Atlantic Ocean. Although Atlantis was just a story, many people over the years have thought that it was real.

LIGHT IT UP

Give each anglerfish a dangling light, like the two below. Then decorate them and color them in!

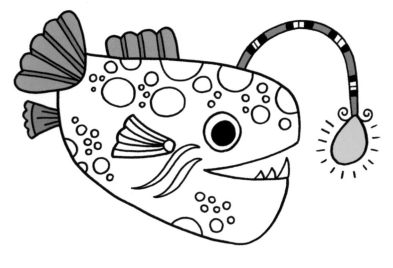

DID YOU KNOW?

Many anglerfish live in the deepest, darkest depths of the ocean, where there is no light. Some anglerfish have a glowing lure attached to the top of their head to attract their prey. By the time their prey realize what the pretty light bobbing in front of them is, it is too late, and the anglerfish snaps them up!

Opulent Octopus

Finish decorating this octopus with beautiful patterns, then color it in.

54

Use the head as a starting point to draw your own octopus. Remember—they have eight arms!

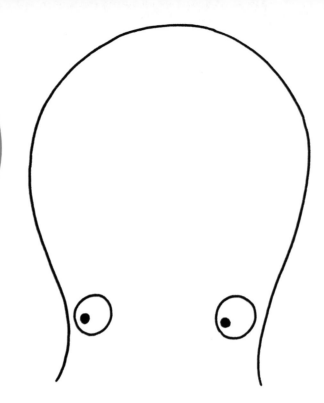

MAKE A FRUITY FISH

Fruits like strawberries, raspberries, blueberries, oranges, and apples are great for making this tasty edible fish. For an optional ocean background, lay fruit over blueberry yogurt in a shallow bowl.

Ask an adult to help you cut up your fruits, and arrange them in a fish shape like the one here!

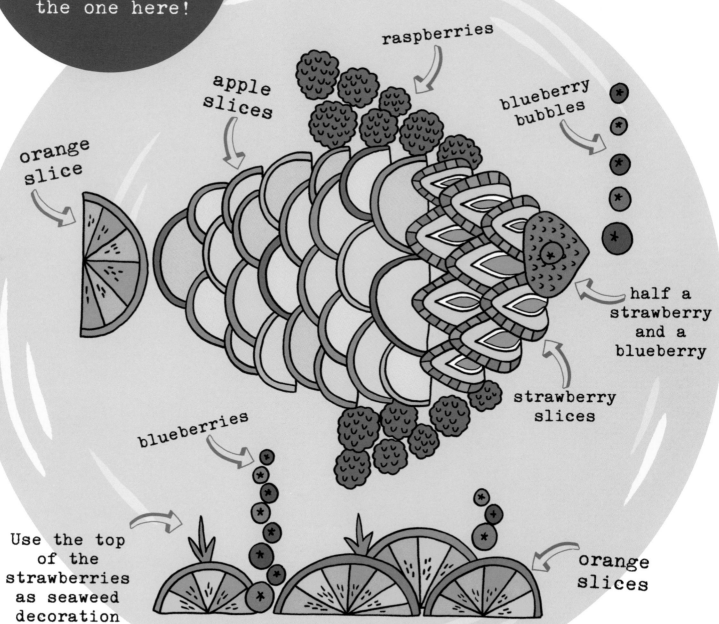

raspberries

apple slices

blueberry bubbles

orange slice

half a strawberry and a blueberry

strawberry slices

blueberries

Use the top of the strawberries as seaweed decoration

orange slices

If you could create your own sea creature, what would it look like? Fins or tentacles, pincers or paws? Does it swim, float, or walk?

Design your own animal in the space below.

MAKING WAVES

All of the words in this puzzle have to do with ocean animals. Use the clues below to complete the puzzle. It's quite a splash!

DOWN:
1. This sea animal makes pearls out of the things that get caught in its shell
2. Spider-like sea animal known for the large claws it uses to defend itself
4. Large sea animal known for its long tusks
5. This rock- and plant-like sea animal provides homes for many of its fellow ocean dwellers
7. Sea animal or the object you use to wash dishes
8. Large fish known for its hunting skills
9. Flightless waddling bird that swims in the southernmost seas
10. Fish that blows up into a ball to defend itself
12. Fish often eaten in sandwiches
14. Another name for starfish
16. Despite its name, _____fish, this transparent, bell-like sea creature does not go well with peanut butter
19. Octopuses and squid use this to defend themselves
20. Long, snake-like fish

ACROSS:
1. Another name for killer whale
3. Flat fish that looks like a kite when it swims across seabeds
6. Eight-armed, super-intelligent sea creature
11. Sea reptile known for its shell
13. Deep-sea fish that lures in prey with its glowing head appendage
15. Some of these massive sea animals are the largest mammals in existence
17. This tiny fish, the sea_____, was named after a certain farm animal it looks like, but unlike its namesake, you can't ride it!
18. Fish known for its long, pointy snout
21. This tiny, shrimp-like animal is extremely important to the ocean because so many other animals eat it

58

ORIGAMI FISH

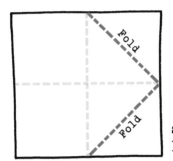

You will need one piece of square paper that is colored on one side and white on the other.

1

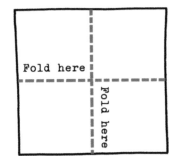

Fold here

Fold here

With the colored side facing down, fold the square in half both ways, then open it up again.

2

Fold

Fold

so it looks like this

Fold the two right corners into the center line.

3

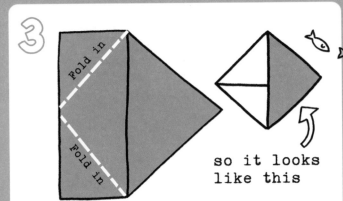

Fold in

Fold in

so it looks like this

Turn the fish over and repeat on the other side. Then turn the fish over again.

4

Fold in

Fold in

so it looks like this

Put your finger on the left corner (circled) and fold the top edge to the center line. Do the same to the bottom. Then turn your fish over.

5

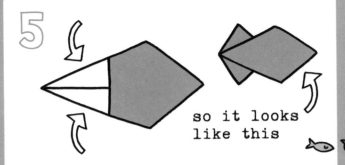

so it looks like this

Fold the flaps back to form a tail. Then turn your fish over.

6

Fold in

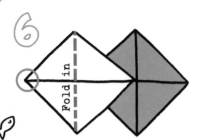

so it looks like this

Take the left corner (circled) and fold the tail back in on itself to the center. Now turn your fish over and draw its face.

INTO THE DEPTHS

Add your face in the submarine window. Then draw what you can see from the submarine!

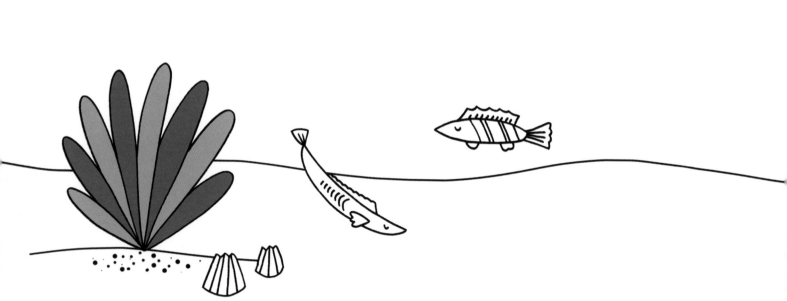

ANSWERS

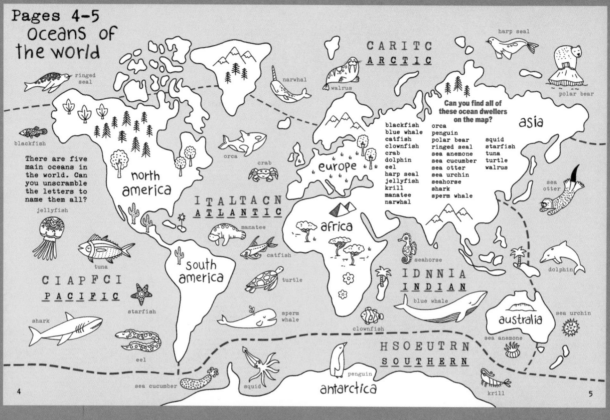

Pages 4-5
Oceans of the world

ringed seal

blackfish

There are five main oceans in the world. Can you unscramble the letters to name them all?

jellyfish

tuna

C I A P F C I
PACIFIC

shark

eel

narwhal

walrus

C A R I T C
ARCTIC

harp seal

polar bear

orca

crab

north america

I T A L T A C N
ATLANTIC

manatee

catfish

europe

Can you find all of these ocean dwellers on the map?

blackfish
blue whale
catfish
clownfish
crab
dolphin
eel
harp seal
jellyfish
krill
manatee
narwhal

orca
penguin
polar bear
ringed seal
sea anemone
sea cucumber
sea otter
sea urchin
seahorse
shark
sperm whale

squid
starfish
tuna
turtle
walrus

asia

sea otter

africa

south america

turtle

starfish

sperm whale

seahorse

I D N N I A
INDIAN

blue whale

clownfish

sea anemone

australia

dolphin

sea urchin

sea cucumber

squid

penguin

antarctica

H S O E U T R N
SOUTHERN

krill

4

5

Page 27
Pearls of Wisdom Maze

START

WHALE WORD SEARCH
Page 30

F X A R P T L Y G O P R N A R W H A L S
K H J E M Q Q T P M A E Y S O M P Z H T
I E P L L I X Z A A L B N V O N A N M M
N E E L A B N H A Z L L Q I O Q L J P M
X F M I Q E U K O C K I U P G F R E T O
P F R K Y M C B E A T L E Q F C Z I V N
G Y U N P O L I L B O F V T Q R K A C T
H H U B H U N A Q O N E S I O P R O P
J X A G W I T W M L W J I R C M Z G I I
S C V J H L B B J M V H C Y A P A E I
K H K P L Q I I O J A A O S G R E G A B
R C L I C A N L Q W Z M D L G N P I E S
A O R P I L O T E R H Y V X E N Y L X D
D K W O N M L L J W E E M W Y E U U C B
F E N D A N G E R E D B A P H G C P E G
B H N I U N C D I K W Q B D A I W M D J
T P T R L M P U J A E R D U U Y V R I A
P Q B K U B Y I S Y A R G O L R P P G E
G S J B T V W R T K M E K K X B W Q S D
B Y U H P M U O I X T H K Y E R U R S D

Number of Krill: 22

62

Page 31
PAIR THE PLANKTON

DID YOU KNOW?
Plankton are mostly microscopic organisms made up of tiny plants and animals. They drift along the ocean currents and are an important source of food for many animals, including the largest animal of all—the blue whale.

Page 40
Seahorse dot-to-dot

Unscramble the letters to name this animal.

O E R E S
H A S

SEAHORSE

Pages 32-33
Match the Mackerel

Match the Mackerel

Here is a shoal of fish, each one different from the next, except two! Can you find the two fish that look exactly alike?

Once you've spotted them, color them in with beautiful matching colors so they stand out! Then color the rest of the fish.

DID YOU KNOW?
A group of fish is called a shoal, but if they're moving together in the same direction, they become a school.

32

33

ANSWERS

TREASURE HUNT Page 49

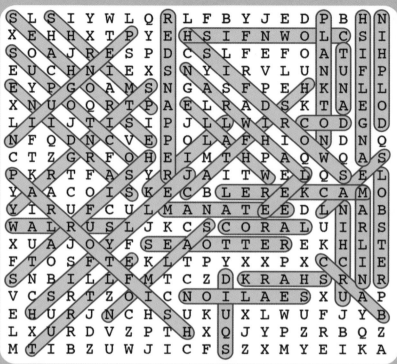

Page 42

Jazzy Jellies!

How many bubbles can you count on this page?

44

Page 58

MAKING WAVES

All of the words in this puzzle have to do with ocean animals. Use the clues below to complete the puzzle. It's quite a splash!

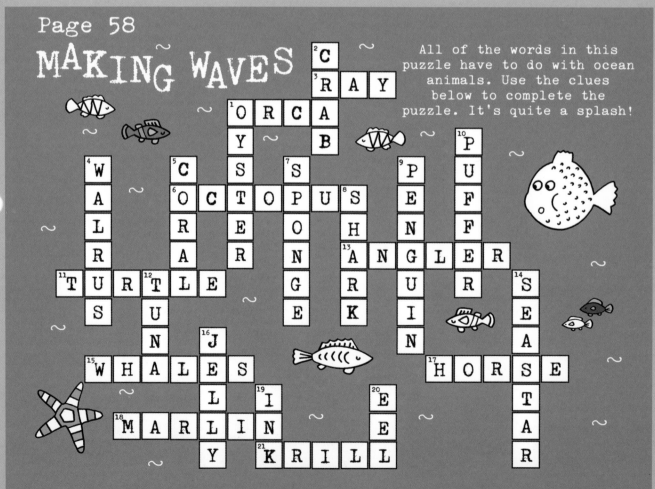